Original title:
The Ocean Calls You

Copyright © 2025 Creative Arts Management OÜ
All rights reserved.

Author: Oliver Bennett
ISBN HARDBACK: 978-1-80581-625-6
ISBN PAPERBACK: 978-1-80581-152-7
ISBN EBOOK: 978-1-80581-625-6

Where the Sky Meets the Sea

The gulls are squawking, what a feat,
They think that fish are a lovely treat.
The sun's a fry pan, sizzling bright,
And everyone's wearing shades that's just right.

The crabs love to dance, oh what a show,
With sideways shuffles and a hard-shell glow.
They wave their claws, such little stars,
While beach balls bounce and rollerboards spar.

Heartbeats in the Current

The jellyfish float like balloons in the sky,
While fish tell tales of those who fly.
Seashells debate who has the best bling,
And seaweed sways, as if it can sing.

A dolphin jumps high, trying to win,
But lands in a wave with a humorous spin.
The octopus winks, eight arms a-flutter,
Saying, 'I know just how to make a splash, like butter!'

Tides of Time's Embrace

The tides come in, with a splish and a splash,
While sandcastles melt in a humorous crash.
The sea is a joker, a whimsical muse,
Playing tag with the wind, what fun to lose!

Seashells giggle as the clams roll their eyes,
Saying, 'Stop it waves, this is a surprise!'
The surfers are trying to balance their boards,
While pufferfish puff up, forgetting their cords.

Anemones in Twilight

The anemones sway with a chuckle and jig,
As the tide pulls in, it's a watery gig.
Starfish congregate for a nightly feast,
Telling tall tales of the mighty beast.

Seahorses prance like they own the whole bay,
While mermaids giggle, as if they might stay.
With laughter that echoes across the deep blue,
The humor of the sea—oh how it grew!

Kaleidoscope of Aquatic Dreams

Bubbles rise like laughter in the tide,
Fish wear sunglasses, they take a ride.
Jellyfish dance in their lovely attire,
While crabs tell jokes at the beach bonfire.

Starfish play poker, oh what a sight,
With seashells betting, it feels just right.
Dolphins flip and share a secret code,
As waves crash in, they lighten the load.

A Driftwood Memoir

Wooden logs, they've got stories to tell,
Like sailing the seas, they've done it so well.
Seagulls gossip about what they've seen,
While starfish chatter about the jelly bean.

A crab with a hat struts down the sand,
Calling the seaweed his biggest fan.
Sardines in suits throw a fancy ball,
As the tide rolls in, they twirl and enthrall.

Beyond the Coral Reefs

Coral castles stand proud in their hue,
As clownfish giggle, what else can they do?
An octopus sketching a portrait of me,
While turtles in bow ties make quite the spree.

Waves play chess with a salty gust,
Sandcastles crumble, but it's a must.
Whales serenade with a booming tune,
While shrimp breakdance under the silver moon.

Vows of the Windswept Sea

Where sand meets the sky, secrets unfold,
Seafoam whispers tales of the bold.
A mural of shells highlighted with glee,
As crabs perform tarantellas, wild and free.

Surfboards line up, a motley crew,
While seabirds manage to steal a shoe.
The waves play charades as they swell and crash,
Floating hello's in a frothy splash.

Untamed Blue Horizons

Waves crash and splash, oh what a sight,
Seagulls steal fries, oh what a fright.
A crab walks sideways, quite the show,
While sunbathers yell, "Hey, watch the flow!"

The sun's too hot, we're starting to fry,
The beach ball bounces, oh me, oh my!
Sand in the sandwiches, what a delight,
The sunburns and giggles continue all night.

Sirens in the Surf

Mermaids with shells sing songs off-key,
They've misplaced their fish; oh, where could it be?
Dolphins doing backflips, oh what a tease,
While jellyfish dance like they're trying to sneeze!

The tide pulls my shorts right off my behind,
As I chase seagulls, they're truly unkind.
Shells clack like castanets in the sun,
While I'm just trying to have a bit of fun!

Embrace of the Deep

Goggles on tight, I dive like a fish,
Only to find a starfish is my wish!
A wave pulls me back, oh what a ride,
With floating noodles, I take my glide!

Flippers stuck in sand, what a sight to see,
I'm chasing my hat, it's run off with a bee!
A seagull squawks loudly, calling my name,
In this watery world, it's all one big game!

Chasing Saltwater Dreams

Buckets and shovels, a castle to build,
But waves take it down, oh, I'm so thrilled!
Sandy ice cream cones drip down my hand,
While the tide pulls my flip-flops into the sand!

Sunburned noses and laughter abound,
A beachday adventure, it's silly, it's sound.
Life's little chaos, like jelly, it sways,
In this sun-kissed place, we'll frolic for days!

The Compass of Time

Pirates set their clocks to chop,
Waves tick-tock as they flip-flop,
Sandy toes and salty ears,
Counting shells instead of years.

Starfish hold the maps so tight,
While crabs dance in the moonlight,
Seagulls sing their silly song,
"Who needs land? We're right where we belong!"

Mermaids blow their conch-shell horns,
Counting fish like dewy morns,
Every splash turns into laughter,
Time floats by, and who's the master?

Yet, if you lose your way to roam,
Just follow the laughter; it leads you home.

Songs from the Ocean Floor

Clams are jamming with a beat,
While plankton dance on tiny feet,
Jellyfish groove in pink and blue,
And seaweed sways with a giggly cue.

Crabs have rock bands made of shells,
Playing tunes that cast funny spells,
The shrimp join in with a trumpet blast,
Music so sweet, it's hard to last.

Octopus strums on a guitar made,
Kelp and coral provide the shade,
Fishes waltz in swirling glee,
The ocean floor's a grand jubilee.

But if you think of a watery snooze,
The sea will giggle—no time to snooze!

Underneath the Seabed

Bubbles rise like tiny dreams,
Beneath the waves, everything beams,
Sand dollars tell their funny tales,
Of seagull pranks and fishy fails.

The shrimp debate if they're too shy,
While sea cucumbers just comply,
Starfish strike a pose so bold,
Winking secrets, stories untold.

Turtles trade their fashion tips,
While dolphins hold their Comedy Scripts,
"Why did the fish blush?" they say,
"Because it saw the ocean spray!"

But deep down where the critters play,
Life's a laugh in every way.

Whispers in the Swell

Seashells whisper secrets low,
"Did you hear about the flow?
A barrel of laughs rolled off a boat,
Now it's a fish's fancy coat!"

Waves tickle what's beneath,
Sandy creatures clasp their teeth,
Bubbles giggle, rippling the sound,
Ocean humor all around.

Gull cackles share a comical jest,
"Why do fish know how to jest?
Because they always have a whale of a time,
Swimming through life in a rhythmic rhyme!"

So tune your ears, the beach is alive,
With giggles and guffaws that always thrive.

The Language of Shells

A seashell speaks in whispers light,
With tales of fish and crabby fights.
It shushes waves, then loudly yells,
   Inviting you to learn its spells.

The conch's snore is quite absurd,
It translates waves in flippy words.
While clams just giggle, stuck in sand,
   In a language we can't understand.

Starfish applaud with wiggly arms,
As dolphins tease with flip-flop charms.
Each grain of sand, a story told,
In a shell's embrace, we find pure gold.

So grab a shell and take a seat,
Join the crowd of creatures sweet.
Their jolly tales are sure to make,
You laugh until your sides all shake.

Triton's Farewell

Triton's waving with a groan,
Leaving behind his watery throne.
He forgot to pack his favorite trinket,
A treasure chest, but no one's seen it!

He dives in for a quick last swim,
But takes the plunge with a silly whim.
His sea-horse cackles, swims away,
'You've lost your mind!' they laugh and play.

Anchors aweigh, oh what a sight,
Triton's flip-flops on too tight.
With bubbles popping at each turn,
He waves goodbye, hoping he'd learn.

Just splash and dash, no looking back,
His ocean friends form a funny pack.
They send him off with laughter loud,
As Triton dives beneath the cloud.

Surrender to the Mist

Fog rolls in with a giggle and squeak,
Hiding fish who prefer to peek.
The seaweed sways with a funny dance,
In this mist, all creatures prance.

Mermaids whisper secrets low,
Wrapped in ribbons, they twirl and flow.
But watch your step, don't lose your shoe,
For the tides might prank you, it's true!

Crabs tap-dance on the sandy floor,
While seagulls squawk, asking for more.
Fish in tuxedos play hide and seek,
In the misty embrace where laughter's peak.

So let the haze wrap tight around,
In giggly waves, we'll laugh and drown.
For in this silliness, one can find,
The wild joy that sea days bind.

Beneath the Surface's Secrets

Bubbles rise like giggles shared,
Fish whisper secrets, feeling bared.
Octopus paints with colors bright,
Creating art in the soft, soft light.

Jellyfish float with a jolly sway,
Tickling each other in a playful play.
While snails boast shells of greatest size,
They march along with sleepy eyes.

Coral reefs hum a pranky tune,
As sea urchins roll this way and that boon.
Underwater, where whimsies thrive,
Fish wear costumes to come alive.

So dive right down and lose your shoes,
In this underwater world, you choose.
For every twist brings joyful dread,
Let the sea be where your smiles spread.

A Mariner's Lament

The captain said to steer and sail,
Yet here I am, caught in a gale.
Fish are laughing, seaweed's a tease,
While I'm tangled up, oh, what a breeze.

Seagulls swoop, stealing my hat,
Chasing my snacks, like a hungry cat.
I thought I'd catch a whale for fun,
But all that's nibbling is my bun!

The compass spins, I lost my way,
A crab waved back, what can I say?
With every wave, my hopes grow small,
This boat's a circus, I'm the fool after all.

But sun's out bright, no need to fret,
With a splash of salt, life's a duet.
I'll fish for laughs and sails for glee,
As the sea plays tricks, just wait and see!

Whirlpools of Memory

Round and round the eddies swirl,
A mermaid's tale, or just a twirl?
I tried to dance, but slipped off the dock,
Now I'm spinning like a silly sock.

The waves are splashing, what a show,
A dolphin giggles with a wink, hello!
Remember when I thought I could dive?
Turns out fish don't like my vibe!

The barnacles whisper, forming a crowd,
As I juggle shells, feeling quite proud.
But every toss leads to a splash,
In this whirlpool dance, I just crash!

Yet every wave that pulls me near,
Brings back laughter, not just fear.
With salty memories, I'll always stay,
In this swirling ocean, come what may!

On Wings of Brine

With a bucket of dreams, I set to glide,
On wings of laughter, through the tide.
A seagull squawks, 'Is that a fry?'
I'd throw her something, but she'd just sigh.

Crabs are prancing, showing their claws,
While fishes chuckle, breaking their jaws.
A jellyfish floats by, oh what a sight,
He's doing the tango—what a delight!

Riding the waves on a surfboard of hopes,
Dancing with dolphins, with silly slopes.
My sunscreen's gone, my nose is bright red,
But hey, that's just how fun can spread!

So here I am, in this splashy spree,
Living my dream, wild and free.
On wings of brine, let troubles wash,
In this giggly world, life's a splash!

Beneath the Glistening Surface

Beneath the waves, where the bubbles pop,
Sea cucumbers lounge, quite a swap.
A clam plays chess with an old starfish,
While I can't find a snack, oh what a wish!

Coral reefs chuckle, giving me grief,
As I struggle to catch, a slippery beef.
I thought I saw treasure, but oh dear me,
Just a rusty old can, all covered in pee!

The anglerfish giggles, his light's too bright,
Giving me ideas, for a late night bite.
But I'm just drifting in this lazy dream,
While everyone's scheming, it's not what it seems.

With creatures around, in this watery zoo,
Each giggle and gurgle feels fresh and new.
So let's raise a glass, or perhaps a shell,
For the fun in the depths, that we know so well!

Moonlit Waves

Under the moon, waves twist and twirl,
Sea creatures dance, give a salty whirl.
A fish with a hat, oh what a sight,
Giggling as seagulls try to take flight.

Barnacles giggle, they're stuck to a rock,
While crabs play tag with a ticking clock.
Starfish wear boots, they strut and strife,
Jellyfish float, living that chill life.

They say there's treasure beneath the spray,
But it's just a flip-flop that's lost its way.
Seagulls squawk jokes, oh how they jest,
Making waves in laughter, we're truly blessed.

Undercurrents of Longing

In the depths, a clam yearns for a mate,
Waving its shell, feeling quite great.
A lonely turtle sings a strange tune,
Dreaming of dances 'neath the full moon.

Octopuses twirl in an endless embrace,
While a crab interrupts with a comedic face.
The fish roll their eyes at the squid's insistence,
But they join in the fun, no need for resistance.

Seaweed sways and joins the ballet,
As dolphins flip, putting on a display.
Anemones blush at the sight of a whale,
Who's cracking up jokes, it's quite a tale!

Chorus of the Gulls

A chorus of gulls with pipes in their beaks,
Singing about sandwiches, and potato leaks.
One sadly lost its bagel today,
It swoops and it swooshes, doing ballet.

They argue and flap, asking who's the best,
A fight over fries in their feathery jest.
One thinks it's funny to snatch a hot fry,
While others just squawk and begin to cry.

Gull's got a selfie with a beachball best,
Under the sun, no time for a rest.
They laugh and they squawk, what a wild crew!
With antics and crazies, staring at you!

A Distinct Ripple

A ripple rolls in from the distant shore,
Carrying secrets of fishy folklore.
"Did you hear 'bout the starfish who walked on its hands?

It won a clapping contest, oh how it stands!"

Mermaids giggle, sipping on seaweed tea,
While sea cucumbers plot to be free.
Every bubble whispers a giggle or two,
Like a whispering joke just for me and you.

The waves chuckle softly, "Come join the dance!"
As seahorses twirl in a splashy romance.
With laughter and splashes, the sea's full of cheer,
Where all are invited, far and near!

Treasures in the Foam

When I dip my toes in the brine,
I find lost sandals, not divine.
A rubber duck waves from afar,
It even brought along a jar.

Seaweed wigs float by with grace,
A crab gives me a friendly face.
I ask it for some fashion tips,
It scuttles off, no time for quips.

A starfish tries to photobomb,
I chuckle—what a silly charm!
Shells sing songs of salty cheer,
In this beach party, all's completely clear.

With treasures found and laughter bright,
The waves roll in with pure delight.
Who knew the sea was such a tease,
A comedy of crustacean ease?

Journey to the Unknown Depths

I grabbed my snorkel and my fins,
Off to find where the sea begins.
Squid turned to me, a goofy grin,
Said, "Under my watch, don't plan to swim!"

A dolphin danced, a silly sight,
With extra flips and a laugh so bright.
"Join the party, don't be a bore!"
As mermaids tap danced on the shore.

Down to the depths, with all my gear,
I met a fish who lent me an ear.
"We tell tales of humans' blunders,
Like when they trip on their own plunders!"

Glowing jellyfish shine like stars,
"Welcome aboard!" they laugh from afar.
We swam and stumbled, a wild spree,
In the deep, where it's funny to be free!

Canvas of the Celestial Sea

Brush strokes of blue in a wobbly dance,
My boat lurches; oh, what a chance!
A seagull scoffs, calls me a clown,
As I paint the waves while upside down.

With every wave, my canvas shifts,
The colors blend with the ocean's gifts.
A starfish critiques my mixing skills,
Says my art's lacking some crabby thrills.

To my right, a schoolfish ensemble,
Singing tunes—oh, how I fumble.
Their scales glint like glittery stars,
While I struggle, just a wannabe czar.

Each brush stroke follows the tide,
In this ocean, I can't decide.
Funny how nature steals the scene,
While I paint, not quite a marine!

Rhythms of the Rolling Surf

The waves crash softly, a starry beat,
Sandals lost; oh, what a feat!
I surf on flippers—what a ride,
While my beach ball laughs, swells with pride.

A seal pops up, offers a cheer,
"Join the fun, never fear!"
In waves of giggles, I tumble and roll,
The surf and I, in one joyful soul.

Sandcastles wobble in a hasty race,
The tide's an artist, full of grace.
With every wave, I chase my hat,
A comedy skit from the ocean fat.

As the tide ebbs, we bid adieu,
The surf whispers secrets, just for me and you.
In laughter's echo, we dance and twirl,
Against the horizon, in a spinning whirl.

Horizon's Embrace

A seagull swooped low, stole my fries,
With a cackle and flap, oh what a surprise!
The waves are like laughter, they bubble and burst,
I'm here for the sun, but the gull's as my first.

Flip-flops are flapping, they dance in the sand,
While sunscreen applies, I'm gobbled up, tanned!
The tide rolls in quick, oh the stories it tells,
But I just want ice cream, can that ocean repel?

A crab with a top hat waltzes on by,
"Care for a dance?" he chirps with a sigh.
I giggle and twirl, though he steps on my toe,
This beach is a circus, with a splash and a show!

As the sun dips low, my cheeks start to glow,
A shadow lurks close, could it be a big show?
But it's just a beach ball, bouncing my way,
With laughter and joy, I'll beach it today!

Voyage to the Abyss

Sailing on waters, so wide and so blue,
I've misplaced my compass, who knew it was due?
The fish they are laughing, they wiggle and sway,
"Your map is upside down!" they jest and they play.

A mermaid with a hangover hums quite a tune,
Her hair full of seaweed, she's lost since noon.
"Hey sailor," she slurs, while sipping on brine,
"I'll guide you to treasure, but first buy me a dine!"

An octopus juggles shells with great flair,
"I've got eight arms, bro, come try if you dare!"
I tumble and fumble, the shells go aglow,
As I slip on a sea sponge, and face-plant below.

The depths are quite murky, the laughter is loud,
Fish throwing a party, it's quite a big crowd.
But all that I want is a soda and sun,
Instead, I find seaweed—guess I better run!

Dancers on the Surf

The waves are all twirling, in a wild ballet,
While I drink my cola, they splash in the spray.
A crab cuts a rug while the sand flies around,
I'm attempting the moonwalk—oh, I'm upside down!

Flip-flops a-flying, the rhythm's a blast,
I've lost both my sandals, oh why not go fast?
The dolphins are giggling, they jump in a line,
And I'm here just flailing, but feeling just fine!

A seagull in shades shows me his best dance,
With moves so outrageous, I can't help but glance.
He nudges me close, to join in the fun,
But all I can manage is to trip and to run!

The tide roars with laughter, a wave takes my hat,
While I leap on the shore like an awkward acrobat.
In this goofy grand show, I'll take my last bow,
For a dance in the salt, is to laugh in the now!

Compass of the Waves

Flipping through maps like I'm finding a dream,
But all I'm really after is an ice cream.
The tides are a puzzle, the currents so bold,
Yet my heart's on a cherry cone, fun to behold!

A dolphin in glasses checks his gold watch,
"Time for a party, your adventure's a scotch!"
But I'm stuck on the deck with a seagull's keen glance,
"Quit stealing my fries! Or join in the dance!"

I hop with the crab as he plays on the shore,
Sandy and happy, I can't help but roar!
The compass is spinning; it's lost in the fun,
While I stick to this thrill like a fish on the run!

As the sun starts to fade, we're painting the sky,
With colors of nonsense, and laughter nearby.
So here's to the waves, in their wavy embrace,
In this silly fool's journey, I've found my true place!

Twilight over the Sea

The sky turns purple, fish start to dance,
A seagull swoops down, took my ice cream by chance.
The crabs are doing a wiggly jig,
While I trip on a wave, feeling quite big.

My shorts are soaked, but who really cares?
I'll just blame the tide, no room for my snares.
The sun dips low, painted like a clown,
Sandy toes giggle, let me not frown.

Flipping flippers, fish in a race,
They laugh at my splashes, oh what a case.
With seaweed hats and shells on parade,
The twilight's a riot, I'm thoroughly swayed.

As darkness falls, the waves start to snore,
With a fizzy sound, they whisper for more.
I wave goodbye to the jumpy finned crew,
But they wink in the moonlight, oh if they only knew!

Songs of the Coral Reef

A fish with a trumpet dances by,
Singing sea shanties, oh me, oh my!
Corals clap shells, a wacky delight,
As turtles groove under the moonlit night.

Starfish strum strings on a kelp guitar,
Crustaceans tap dance, oh what a star!
The jellyfish sway, in a scientific trend,
While octopuses jam, with limbs that extend.

But wait, what's this? A clam turns shy,
It shells up tight, with a soft little sigh.
The fish all cheer, 'Come join the fun!'
But it's hard to dance when your home weighs a ton!

So, with bubbles and laughs, the sea goes round,
With each silly song, joy's easily found.
They bubble over laughter, and who can resist?
When the creatures of the reef have a jam session bliss!

The Blue Horizon Beckons

Over the waves, there's a sign that reads,
"Surf's up, wipeouts are all that you need!"
But in my last dive, I tangled my feet,
With seaweed that giggled, a slippery treat.

Pelicans joke, as they dive for their prey,
"Watch out for the splashes," they cheekily say.
The dolphins join in, flipping with glee,
"Welcome to the circus, come splash with me!"

But my board took a turn, right under a boat,
And there went my snack, does a fish ever gloat?
Seagulls snicker, as I flounder around,
In the realm of blue, hilarity's found.

And as I resurface with a dramatic flair,
The horizon laughs back, windswept and bare.
With a wink and a shake, I jump back to play,
For every wild wave, it's a comical day!

Embrace of the Endless Blue

The sea wraps around like a warm, cozy blanket,
While I search for treasures, or do I even rank it?
Flip-flops abandoned, I rush to the shore,
Chasing the gulls, oh, what a silly chore!

The tide pulls at my shins, waves tickle and tug,
As fish join in laughing, feeling quite smug.
A crab offers advice, "Just sidestep and swing!"
While I'm left tangled—what a peculiar fling!

Watching barnacles judgmentally gaze,
As I blunder about in this salty maze.
But a quick splash of water and a twist of my fate,
Turns the grumpy barnacles into my great mates.

So here I will stay, under skies so benign,
With slapstick moments and laughter divine.
Together we'll form an uproarious crew,
In the embrace of the blue, life's giggles ensue!

Dance of the Rolling Waves

Waves giggle and they splash,
Doing the twist, oh what a bash!
Seagulls join with their silly cries,
As crabs dance with wiggling thighs.

On surfboards, the fish all glide,
Wearing sunglasses, full of pride.
A dolphin shows its finest moves,
While octopuses bust some grooves.

Beachballs bounce and everyone plays,
Sandy toes in a sunlit haze.
A clam starts a limbo contest,
And you can't help but feel so blessed.

When the tide pulls back, they cheer,
For the next wave's drawing near.
With laughter echoing through the foam,
The sea feels just like a home.

Beneath the Celestial Sea

Stars twinkle like fish on a charm,
Bubbles pop with a funny alarm.
A starfish starts a wiggly dance,
While jellyfish float in a trance.

Crabs in suits sip on their drink,
Underwater, they chat and think.
"Do you remember last Tuesday's mess?
That wave made quite the hairy dress!"

Mermaids laugh with shells in their hair,
Making puns like they don't have a care.
With clamshell phones and gossip galore,
Who knew the sea was never a bore?

As waves crash down, the party goes on,
The fun in the tides is never quite gone.
So come on down, take a dive,
And dance with the fish, so lively and alive!

Secrets of the Briny Deep

Beneath the waves, secrets unfold,
As fish tell tales that are silly and bold.
A turtle wears googles, thinks it's quite cool,
While sea urchins insist that they're no fool.

The octopus tells a knock-knock joke,
Making even the dullest fish choke.
"Knock, knock," it says with a wavy grin,
"Who's there?" giggles the clownfish with fin.

Pearls tucked away in an oyster's shell,
Are treasures that whisper and giggle as well.
"Who knew the sea could be filled with glee?
Come dive into laughter and swim over me!"

With shrimps that wear tiny top hats,
And a fish who believes it can chat with the bats.
Secrets abound in this watery space,
Where everyone's smiling, a laugh on their face.

Lullabies of the Shoreline

The sun dips low, the sky turns pink,
While crickets chirp and sea lions wink.
A gentle wave hums a soothing tune,
As children giggle under the moon.

Sandcastles built with the silliest flair,
With all kinds of shells piled up with care.
The tide sings softly, with a wink and a nod,
While frolicking fish give a cheeky applaud.

Seagulls squawk like they've lost their map,
As kids in the surf take a quick splashy nap.
The world feels light in the sweet salty air,
Where the shorelines bubble with laughter to share.

So drift to sleep with the waves as your guide,
In dreams of the sea, where the funny fish glide.
Let the lullabies carry you far away,
To a shore where silliness rules every day.

Whispers of the Tides

Crabs dance around in their tiny suits,
While fish gossip 'bout their daily hoots.
A dolphin pops up, gives a cheeky grin,
Says, "Join the splash; it's a laugh, let's begin!"

Seagulls squawk jokes, they can't be contained,
One steals a sandwich, the beachgoers complained.
But foolishness reigns as the waves start to roll,
Come here for a giggle, the tide takes its toll!

Sandcastles topple with a cloudy cheer,
As the tide shouts loudly, "Look, I'm still here!"
Buckets and spades get whisked out to play,
In a world of silliness, come laugh, get away!

So dive in this laughter, don't be so shy,
With shells as your props, let's give it a try.
From the humor of waves, we won't dare to flee,
Let's dance with the currents, oh goofy spree!

Sirens of the Sea

Mermaids with sass sing tunes out of tune,
Their scales sparkle bright, a dazzling cartoon.
One slips on a starfish, takes a wild dive,
"Why can't I walk? I can't seem to thrive!"

Crab chorus cracks up with a pinch of delight,
While a jellyfish boogies under pale moonlight.
"Catch me if you can!" a sly fish does shout,
But the squid's silly dance leaves everyone out.

Seashells are gossiping, oh what a scene,
"Did you hear about Sally? She's gone quite marine!"
Laughter erupts as they splash and they play,
In this silly sea, it's a fun cliché!

So come join the frolic, leave worries ashore,
With laughter abounding, who could ask for more?
As waves of giggles spill over the sand,
These sirens will promise that fun's always planned!

Beneath Waves of Blue

Bubbles rise up with a chuckle and fizz,
Fish plan a grand party; they're all in a whizz.
An octopus juggles, oh what a sight,
With party hats on, they dance through the night!

Seashells start spinning, caught up in the groove,
While sea urchins wobble, no way they can move!
Whales play a game of tag deep in the sea,
"Catch me if you can!" Oh, what glee there will be!

The starfish applaud, giving claps with their arms,
"Your moves are fantastic, your style has its charms!"
Turtles play limbo, making waves to the beat,
In this deep underwater, it's just pure retreat!

With laughter and bubbles, the spree won't end,
The ocean's a playground, a true loyal friend.
So dive into joy with a splash and a cheer,
Beneath waves of blue, happiness is near!

Echoes of Salt and Sand

Footprints in sand tell tales of the day,
While crabs plot their heists in a sneaky ballet.
The wind whispers secrets that tickle the shore,
As gulls try to find out just what's in store!

A clam tells a joke that no one can hear,
"Why did the seaweed break up? It had too much fear!"
The waves are reciting a comedy show,
With giggles and splashes, the laughter will flow.

Sandcastles wobble with every high tide,
As children just laugh, with jewels in their pride.
A conch shell's confession, its voice comes alive,
"I'm up for a chat, let's see who can jive!"

Together we'll tumble in this beachy delight,
With echoes of laughter, extending the night.
So come join the joy, don't sit idly bland,
In the echoes of salt and the warmth of the sand!

Rhapsody of the Sea Foam

Waves are dancing, making a splash,
Seagulls are laughing, oh what a clash!
The fish wear hats, it's quite a sight,
As starfish boogie, in the moonlight.

Crabs in tuxedos, they waddle on sand,
Their tiny steps, truly unplanned.
Beach balls bounce, like they're on a spree,
Join the party, it's wild and free!

The sunset's a painter, with colors so bright,
It spills on the water, what a delight!
Don't forget your beach towel, or you'll be shocked,
When the tide comes in and your phone gets docked.

Here comes a dolphin, with tricks to show,
He flips and he flops, putting on a show.
Grab some popcorn and take a seat,
It's oceanic comedy, truly a treat!

Horizons of Endless Blue

The sky is a canvas, so vast and wide,
With clouds shaped like ducks, oh, what a ride!
The sun wears glasses, looking so cool,
While jellyfish swim in their own little pool.

Pirates pass by, looking for gold,
But all they found was a whale that was bold.
He winked at the captain, and with a splash,
Stole their treasure and made quite a dash!

Sandy the crab, he's building a throne,
With seashells and sand, he's not alone.
His royal court giggles, a silly sight,
When a wave crashes down, what a great fright!

Kites fly over, in colors galore,
As children chase them, yelling for more.
Laughter and joy, fill the salty breeze,
Who knew the coast could be such a tease!

Mermaids in the Mist

Mermaids are gossiping, tales to spin,
Of fish with legs, and of fish with fin!
They comb their long hair, made of seaweed,
And giggle at sailors who take the lead.

A sea cucumber wears a monocle tight,
In his little world, he feels quite right.
With turtles in bowties, they march in a line,
Claiming that seabeds are simply divine!

Octopus refuse to play any games,
Too busy ink-squirting and making new names.
Their parties are wild, with poses that sizzle,
You might get tangled, if you dare to drizzle!

Under the moonlight, they flip and they twirl,
With bubbles as pearls, they dance and they swirl.
So if you hear laughter, don't be too brusque,
Join the mermaids, in the evening's dusk!

Secrets in the Seashell

Seashells are whispering secrets untold,
Of treasures hidden, and strange things gold.
A clam with a crown, he's quite the sight,
He rules the tide pool, with all of his might!

Seagulls are mailmen, delivering news,
Of beach gossip, and odd little blues.
They squawk and they squabble, taking their flight,
While crabs debate if sand is too bright!

There's a treasure map drawn in ketchup and fries,
Leading to spots where the laughter does rise.
Join the search party, we'll dig with our hands,
For buried pizza, that's just what life demands!

The waves hum a tune, that tickles our ears,
A melody sweet, that wipes all our fears.
So lean in closely, and hear them out,
For life at the shore, is what fun's all about!

Calligraphies of the Coast

Seagulls squawk like they own the place,
While crabs march in their armored grace.
Sandcastles lean, a noble flop,
As waves come in, they go kerplop!

Flip-flops flying through the salty air,
Tangled hair and sunscreen everywhere.
A jellyfish floats like a fancy balloon,
Saying, "Come dance to my wobbly tune!"

Shimmering Secrets Beneath.

Fish in tuxedos, oh what a sight,
Throwing a party in the moonlight.
Octopus juggling, seaweed on a string,
Who knew the deep was a quirky fling?

Starfish gossiping over a shellfish feast,
Laughing at the clam who's quite the beast.
Shrimp in shades, looking ultra cool,
While turtles swim back to their school!

Whispers of the Tide

Waves like whispers with a silly tone,
Telling stories of fish with a moan.
Sand dollars giggle when the tide is low,
As beach balls bounce in a summer glow.

Seashells gossip, sharing their plans,
"Let's dance!" they shout, "in tides and sands!"
With every roll, a chuckle is found,
In this watery world that spins 'round and 'round!

Echoes Beneath the Waves

Watermelon sharks swim with a grin,
Diving deep to play peek-a-boo again.
Barnacles bragging of their grand home,
While pufferfish puff out, "Don't you know I'm foam?"

On this sandy stage, it's a merry jest,
Mermaids laughing, giving fish a quest.
Crabs in slippers dance without a care,
Making waves, for they're debonair!

Heartbeats of Marine Life

Fish sing songs in a bubbly choir,
They tickle the seaweed with thin wire.
Crabs wear hats made of shiny shells,
While dolphins dance, ringing joyful bells.

A clam dreams big of a bright new day,
As seagulls plot to steal his buffet.
Starfish lounge on the sandy beach bed,
While octopuses juggle with their head.

Whales throw parties with splashes and splorps,
While tiny shrimp play tiny little sports.
The tide rolls in with a goofy grin,
And sea cucumbers twirl, let the fun begin!

Jellyfish be bop on the rhythm divine,
While bubble-blowing squids spill their fine wine.
So dive on in, let's take on this spree,
And laugh with the waves, just you and me!

Requiem for a Distant Shore

A lonely wave whined about its plight,
Missing a seagull for a winged fright.
Shells echo stories of fishy romance,
While crabs on the beach break into a dance.

Sandcastles crumble, but that's just fine,
As tourists compete on a stand-up line.
Starfish sing ballads, all out of tone,
With mermaids laughing from seaweed throne.

A whale tries to tell a dad joke or two,
But sea turtles roll their eyes, oh boohoo!
They say every wave has a laugh or a cry,
As jellyfish giggle and float by and by.

So raise up your flippers and join this parade,
With fish in tuxedos, a splashy charade.
For every bad pun, there's a smile so wide,
On this distant shore, where the fun won't hide!

In the Embrace of the Blue

Dolphins wear sun hats to stay nice and cool,
While angelfish swim like they rule the pool.
Crabs ride the surf on a boogie board,
As sea urchins cheer, "You're never ignored!"

Waves toss about with wild, silly flair,
While turtles contemplate who's got the best hair.
Seahorses spin tales of love from a child,
In the embrace of the blue, laughter's so wild.

The plankton throw parties for fish on the run,
As stingrays practice their newest dance fun.
Eels tangled up in a knot just to tease,
While fish in tuxedos are sure to appease.

So come join the fun, bring your oceanic cheer,
Grab a shell phone, let's make this clear.
For in the deep blues, where the laughter survives,
We'll swim through the tides, where the humor thrives!

Marshlands and Mysterious Depths

In marshy lands where the frogs do croak,
A gator grins, sharing one of his jokes.
Moss hangs their hats on the trees waving low,
While turtles roll by, enjoying the flow.

The herons strike poses as if on a stage,
While otters perform like they're free from a cage.
With every splash, a new giggle is heard,
From ducks wearing bowties, it's simply absurd!

In mysterious depths where the darkness dips,
A fish with a flashlight takes glamorous trips.
Around him, friends swim, in colors so bright,
Making sure every shadow is filled with delight.

So come take a peek through the reeds, oh so grand,
Where critters exchange their best jokes on the sand.
In marshlands and depths where the laughter is deep,
Join in the fun, take a leap off the heap!

Soliloquy of the Seafarer

Oh salty breeze, you tease my hair,
I lost my sandwich, floating out there.
With waves like giants, my boat's a toy,
I scream 'ahoy' while the seagulls enjoy.

Fish swim by, laughing in glee,
They see my dance, then flee from me.
I wave my arms, but they just chuckle,
Turns out, fish don't like my belly's shuffle.

The sun shines bright, I slip and slip,
On wet decks, I take a dive trip.
With a splash and a plop, my hat takes flight,
As the crabs snicker at my comical plight.

Nautical life, a jester's dream,
With barnacles climbing, it's the ultimate scheme.
Laughing waves mock my hearty cheer,
But I'll keep sailing, for there's fun right here.

Tranquility on the Water's Edge

Waves roll in with a bubbly cheer,
I stumble on rocks, oh dear, oh dear!
With seashells lost and flip-flops tossed,
I'm trying to balance, but at what cost?

A crab waves hello, pinching my toe,
While dolphins snicker at my wobbly show.
Sandcastles crumble with each little tide,
As I try to build, but the tide just glides.

Seagulls glide past, wearing their shades,
I try to impress—oh, what charades!
They steal my chips, oh what a fuss,
While I'm left with crumbs, what a bust!

But laughter's the language of all seaside,
Even if I've lost my sense of pride.
So I dance with the waves, and sing with the breeze,
A jester at heart, doing just as I please.

Letters in the Sand

Writing my name in the soft, warm sand,
A wave sneaks up—oh! That wasn't planned!
It laughs as it washes my letters away,
Guess I'll start over—oh well, play by play.

I scribbled a heart, a smiley for fun,
The tide roars back—oh no! It's begun!
It giggles and twirls, my art is erased,
I chase it in vain, no time to be paced.

Sandy messages drawn with delight,
Come springing and swooshing, oh what a sight!
I can't keep up with this rascally tide,
It's a mischievous partner; I can't let it slide.

But still, I keep writing, letters galore,
Maybe a poem? A treasure to store!
Each wave a reminder of laughter's embrace,
As I leap and I dodge for just a small space.

Tempests and Tranquility

The skies get dark, and the winds start to howl,
My boat sways wildly—a real sea growl!
With a squawk and a splash, my hat takes flight,
I'm just a sailor, losing this fight.

A tempest whirls as I cling to the mast,
I holler and yell, hoping the storm will pass.
But deep in the chaos, a flicker of glee,
As I whirl and twirl, like a fish set free.

But wait! What's that? A calm in the air,
The sea's serenade is a gentle affair.
My heart's still racing, but laughter is near,
As I spin in the stillness with boisterous cheer.

With friends by my side, we dance on the deck,
Kites of the clouds fly wild with respect.
For storms may come, they'll hush and retreat,
But the laughter we gather is oh-so sweet.

A Salty Serenade

The waves are winking, oh so bright,
Fish are giggling, what a sight!
Seagulls squawk in a silly dance,
As crabs do the cha-cha, take a chance!

Flip-flops flying, oh what a thrill,
Sunburned noses, holiday chill.
In the tide pool, sea stars grin wide,
As children squeal, on a slippery ride!

The sandy castles, tall and proud,
Tumble like dreams, under a cloud.
Seaweed hairdos, such a fun trend,
"Whale hello!" we yell, as the waves blend!

So grab your floaties, join the fun,
Splashing and laughing, we won't be done.
With laughter echoing across the bay,
It's a silly sea party, hip-hip-hooray!

Journey to the Abyss

In a tiny boat with a wibbly wheel,
We try to capture a tuna meal.
My friend lost his hat to the breeze,
Now it's a fish's favorite tease!

Dolphins pop up to say hello,
I think they're laughing at our show.
Tiny octopuses play hide and seek,
While we're out here, feeling rather bleak!

The compass spins; it's quite a mess,
As we navigate this watery stress.
A crab in a suit gives us a tour,
"Follow me! I know a great adventure!"

But suddenly, the boat starts to sway,
And we scream "What's the right way?"
With laughter bubbling like the sea,
Who knew swimming in chaos could be so free?

Reflections on the Sea's Canvas

The sea paints pictures, wild and bright,
With fish that sparkle like jewels in light.
But wait! What's that? A floating shoe,
A masterpiece made just for you!

Mermaids giggle, their hair all wrong,
Too much seaweed? They sing a new song!
With every splash, laughter entwines,
As crabs play the drums on the sandy lines!

Underwater selfies, what a delight,
With jellyfish filters, oh what a sight!
"Look, I caught a wave!" yells a kid in glee,
While seagulls photobomb, "Hey, look at me!"

You'd swear the tides had a comedic touch,
With waves that twist and crash just too much.
As we float on laughter, the sun goes down,
The sea's quirky canvas, forever renown!

Call of the Horizon

While sailing towards the setting sun,
I thought I heard a fish say, "Run!"
To seagulls grinning with witty flair,
"Don't forget to pack your seaweed hair!"

The horizon sparkles with secrets untold,
As fishing rods dance with stories bold.
But each tug on the line feels like a tease,
With fish giving me a hearty squeeze!

We met a whale with a magical hat,
Who told the best jokes while sitting flat.
"Why don't fish play piano?" it asked with glee,
"Because you can't tuna fish, you see!"

So here's to adventures where laughter flows,
With crabby companions and sun-kissed toes.
As we sail the waves with a heart full of cheer,
Let every splash echo the joy we hold dear!

Beneath the Sailor's Star

Under a star that's twinkling bright,
A sailor's hat takes off in flight.
Fish look up with a cheeky grin,
As the captain searches for a mermaid's fin.

Seagulls squawk with a comical flair,
While the salty breeze messes up his hair.
Waves dance and splash, oh what a scene,
As he tries to balance on that canteen.

The compass spins like a hula hoop,
He shouts, 'Land ho!' while spilling his soup.
With each wave that comes crashing through,
The boat laughs as if it too needs a brew.

So here's to those beneath the stars,
Who navigate life like sailing cars.
With laughter and jests they set out anew,
In search of treasure and a laugh or two!

Rhythms of the Shore

The beach is calling, with a funny sound,
As crabs dance sideways all around.
Seashells giggle, rolling on the sand,
While jellyfish float like they've got a band.

Waves tickle toes and chase them back,
Sandcastles crumble like a snack attack.
Seagulls mime with exaggerated flair,
'Look at us, we fly without a care!'

Kids jump in puddles, splashing with glee,
While sunscreen's smeared in the shape of a bee.
The sun winks down with a grin quite cheeky,
As the tide comes in, oh so sneaky.

So let the rhythms of laughter soar,
With each wave crashing upon the shore.
In this silly dance that nature drew,
Life's a beach party; enjoy the view!

Land of Make-Believe and Water

In a land where mermaids hold tea parties,
And dolphins do tricks like spunky smarties.
A pirate on stilts, he wobbles around,
As fish play poker on the playground ground.

The sunfish wears a top hat so grand,
While octopuses juggle with their own hand.
Floating on noodles, a whale sings a tune,
As sea turtles dance beneath the bright moon.

The water is laughter, the waves are the beat,
Where everyone's dancing with fins on their feet.
Join the parade of silliness abound,
In this wacky place where joy can be found.

So dive into fun, where the playful dwell,
In this land of make-believe, all's well!
Each splash is a giggle, each dive is a play,
Where every fish wishes you'd come and stay!

Horizon's Gentle Embrace

A horizon stretches with a wink so sly,
Where boats chase sunsets that giggle and fly.
The sky throws colors like it's in a spree,
While the waves chuckle 'come play with me!'

A floating log acts as a silly throne,
For a crab wearing shades, feeling quite grown.
The tides get giddy, swaying side to side,
As they serenade fish in a watery glide.

With seagulls serenading forgotten songs,
The sea laughs softly, 'You can't go wrong!'
Pirate parrots join in with funny squawks,
While sandpipers dance in their beachy frocks.

So grab your hats, let's relish the chase,
Where joy is abundant in this ocean space.
With every gentle wave, a story in place,
As we tumble through laughter in horizon's embrace!

Dreams Carried by the Tide

A sandcastle built, but it's a mistake,
Seagulls swoop down, for a piece of my cake.
Flip-flops on sideways, I stumble in glee,
Maybe I should've just stayed with the tea.

Waves like DJ's, they spin and they twist,
My towel's a boat, oh, how could I resist?
Sunburned my nose, I named it 'Rudolph'.
The ocean's my friend, though it makes me scoff.

Fishing for laughs, but caught a shoe instead,
To my surprise, it had more style, I said.
Laughter erupts, as I dance on the pier,
The tide pulls me in, I'll conquer my fear.

Here comes a wave, I'm ready to splash,
I'll ride it like thunder, just look at me dash!
Maybe next time I'll stay out of the way,
But for now, let's have fun! Hip-hip-hooray!

Driftwood Tales

A stick floats by, it tells me a rhyme,
It says it's been drifting since old ancient time.
With shells for a crown, it reigns with such pride,
Saying, 'Join me for tales!' as it wobbles with tide.

A fish swims past, looking shocked at my style,
I wave my hands wildly, it pauses a while.
"You dance like a seaweed blown by the breeze!
Better than my cousins, who swim just to tease!"

A crab pulls a stunt, it scuttles and rolls,
I'm laughing so hard, it's stealing my shoals.
Together we prank, creating a show,
While dolphins nearby are all cheering 'hooray!'

Sunset's our backdrop, painting the floor,
A driftwood forever, I shan't ask for more.
In this sea of stories, we play and we bow,
I'll drift right alongside, we'll take a fun vow!

Where the Sea Meets the Sky

At the edge of the world, don't take life too serious,
Where gulls joke around, and clouds are delirious.
I tried to build wings, they looked like a mess,
Yet off I went flapping, just feeling the stress.

The waves are hummed tunes, that make me wiggle,
While crabs hold a party and dance with a jiggle.
Splashing around, I challenge the tide,
But it just laughs back, with a watery glide.

The sky drops confetti, from clouds full of glee,
As I chase the horizon, what will it be?
A smile from a fish, or a wink from the sun?
Whatever it is, I'll say, "Bring it on, fun!"

So here I go shouting, I'm free and I'm loud,
Dancing with fishes, I feel so proud.
Where the sea meets the sky, is where I belong,
With giggles and splashes, we'll sing our own song!

Call of the Wind-Swept Shore

The wind whispers secrets, with a laugh in its tone,
It tickles my hair, 'Come on, let's roam!'
With flip-flops in hand, I stumble around,
Can't find my balance, why is it so round?

Shells talk in riddles, they giggle and tease,
Saying, "Grab the sand, come dance with the breeze!"
I twirl with a starfish, we're best friends today,
And the crab shouts, "Dance! Don't worry, just play!"

Paddling my feet as the tide starts to rise,
I swear I just saw, a fish wink with surprise!
I chase down the sand, it flicks like a rogue,
I should've worn sneakers, or stuck to a frog.

Laughing with joy, running wild, it's my wish,
Every creature joins in, the sea's quite the dish.
So off we go, trailing laughter and cheer,
On this wind-swept shore, it's fun that we steer!

The Dream of Anchored Souls

In a boat that creaks and sways,
Fish slap their fins in a silly daze.
Sailors dream of treasure,
But find only stinky fish pleasure.

With a parrot perched on a head,
Squawking worries, raising dread.
The stars above are just for show,
While the waves dance to a silly flow.

Every splash is a secret laugh,
As crabs do a silly photograph.
Flip-flops fly with each wild wave,
An anchored soul? Not that brave!

So we sip our drinks from plastic cups,
While debating which way the seagull jumps.
The sun may set, the fish may bore,
But we'll just giggle, then ask for more.

Journey Through the Nautilus

Inside a shell, so snug and tight,
A snail takes off with all its might.
Waves whoosh by in a funny race,
As jellyfish float with an elegant grace.

Octopus joins with tentacle flair,
Pulling pranks with a silly air.
Squid play tag with a splash and squawk,
While starfish lounge like they're on a dock.

In this wild underwater spree,
Crabs put on a rock concert, you see!
They tap-dance on sand, oh what a sight,
Their music's so good, they're up all night.

But fear not the dark, silly gales,
For dolphins splash in their happy trails.
They wink and tease, swim in loops,
As we all chuckle with our flippy flops.

Ebb and Flow of Memories

Waves roll in, bringing tales of old,
Like a family photo that's tinged with bold.
Uncle Bob swims with a bright red hat,
While Grandma's floatie looks like a cat.

Family beach days, sunburnt glee,
With sand in the snacks, oh woe is me!
We bury our toes, and complain of sand,
While laughing at seagulls, our big demand.

Each wave that crashes brings back the laughs,
Of sunscreen battles and silly gaffes.
Belly flops and awkward dives,
Joking that this is how fun survives!

As the tide flows back and forth with glee,
We collect seashells as a family spree.
Laughter echoes along the shore,
A funny tale we will always adore.

Cry of the Lighthouse Keeper

A keeper stands in a hat so tall,
Shouting to ships with a loud 'y'all!'
But they can't hear him through the mist,
So he makes silly faces, with a clenched fist.

The beam spins round with dizzy delight,
Guiding lost boats through the night.
Yet each vessel rolls their eyes and laughs,
As the keeper juggles his quirky staffs.

He waves and giggles, what a sight,
As a pelican steals his snack at night.
'Hey! Come back!', he shouts in hot pursuit,
While seagulls cackle, enjoying the loot.

With each wacky dance and comic pose,
His lighthouse beams, nobody knows.
In this silly realm, where laughter rings,
Every sea creature shares his flings.

Rising with the Waves

When the surf comes crashing down,
My sandals take a swim, oh no!
I chase them like a playful hound,
While seagulls laugh in the show.

Sand gets stuck in every fold,
Ice cream melts in the warm sunlight.
My beach chair turns to a throne,
But the wind steals my hat, quite a sight!

With each wave, a giggle bursts,
Splashing water, what a game!
I tumble in, the sea, it thirsts,
And calls me back, yet again, the same!

Oh, salty breeze, you tickle me,
With jellyfish doing a waltz.
Caught in a tide of glee, you see,
Each wave is a whirlpool of fun and faults!

Galaxy of the Sea

Starfish surfing on the waves,
Count them all, there's quite a lot!
Shells that seem to misbehave,
Planning my beach party plot.

Crabs in their tiny cars, zooming,
Bikini-clad, they drive with glee.
Gulls in the crowd, they're crooning,
To the rhythm of the sea's decree.

Load those snacks, the picnic's set,
And watch a dolphin do a flip.
When it lands, you won't forget,
The moment skips like a popcorn trip!

Eels in tuxedos joining in,
Throwing seaweed like confetti.
Dance with them, and let's begin,
This cosmic party is all ready!

Shimmering Reflections

Mirrors made of ocean spray,
Remind me of last year's pie fight.
With a splash, my shoes betray,
As I laugh 'till the stars ignite.

Fish wearing sunglasses pass by,
Sardines throwing epic cheering.
They say it's a watery high,
But all I get is salty sneering.

With each wave that rolls ashore,
I find a crab with my lost sock.
Caught in its claws, I can't ignore,
The beach has turned into a mock!

My friends join in, a shining crew,
With beach balls flying far and wide.
We giggle beneath the sky so blue,
And ride the waves like an ocean glide!

Odyssey of Tides

A flip-flop's fate beneath the sun,
It sails away like a dream unfurled.
My sea monster friend just had his fun,
Now he's plotting to steal my world.

I try to catch a shrimp for supper,
But they dodge like evasive spies.
With every splash, I'm turning flopper,
And end up chasing seagull lies.

The waves shout jokes, a liquid thrill,
While barnacles tap dance on my feet.
I tumble down, it's such a chill,
And fish giggle as they take a seat.

On this journey through salty laughter,
The tides swirl joy, a playful spree.
I wave goodbye and chase after,
The ocean's whimsy, wild and free!

www.ingramcontent.com/pod-product-compliance
Lightning Source LLC
Chambersburg PA
CBHW072130070526
44585CB00016B/1603